S E C T I O N   I

Introduction

1.1 In March 1996, I reported to the Secretaries of State for Education and Employment, for Wales and for Northern Ireland on the framework of qualifications for 16–19 year olds. This is a summary of that Report. It contains my main recommendations. The full Report gives a complete statement of the recommendations and the rationale for them. It also contains a summary of views and findings from the extensive consultation and research undertaken since July 1995. The terms of reference and purposes of the Review are given in Appendix 1.

1.2 The Report proposes a coherent national framework, covering all the main qualifications and the achievements of young people at every level of ability. It goes beyond that, to recognise achievement outside the main formal qualifications, as part of a restructured and relaunched National Record of Achievement. Because the qualifications appropriate for 16–19 year olds are relevant to people of all ages, it takes into account the needs of adults, particularly those studying part-time. It identifies barriers to achievement and ways to deal with them.

1.3 Stability is important, so the proposed national framework is based on the present qualifications. But it seeks to bring the structure of A levels and the General National Vocational Qualification (GNVQ) into close alignment. This is to enable students to build up a portfolio of qualifications across both pathways. It proposes the renaming of the Advanced GNVQ as the "Applied A level".

1.4 The Report argues that the structure of bodies for regulating and making awards should reflect the recent merger of the Government's responsibilities for education and training into the Department for Education and Employment (DfEE). This will help to bring greater coherence into the framework of qualifications, and challenge pervasive attitudes inherited from the past towards the relative worth of achievement in the academic and vocational pathways.

1.5 The Report responds to the representations by employers on the need to build up competence in the key skills of communication, the application of number and information technology, as well as to their concerns to see young people develop wider skills such as team-working, problem-solving and managing their own learning.

1.6 It gives explicit recognition and support through the qualifications system to the National Targets for Education and Training.

1.7 Following the report of the National Commission on Education, it also encourages an option for post-16 education that combines depth of study with breadth. A high level of achievement in communication, the application of number and information technology is a precondition of the proposed award.

1.8 The Report proposes a new approach to Youth Training and its relaunch with a new national identity.

1.9 It addresses concerns about the rigour of A levels, and welcomes the proposals to improve GNVQs and National Vocational Qualifications (NVQs), made in the Capey and

Beaumont reviews, with which I co-operated during the work leading to this Report.

1.10 The Report gives support to the development of a strengthened GNVQ as a major alternative to A levels, and as a means of providing the underpinning knowledge and understanding for broad occupational areas, and progression to NVQs. It seeks to encourage young people across the whole ability range to consider the options now available for combining work with part-time study for NVQ qualifications, from the age of 16.

1.11 Through a range of proposals, including a new Advanced Subsidiary qualification, the restructuring of the GNVQ, and high quality advice to young people on the choices they have to make, the Report seeks to reduce the present high levels of non-completion and wastage in post-16 education. These proposals seek thereby to help learners get recognition for their achievements, and secure more effective use of public resources.

1.12 While the Report is primarily concerned with those aged between 16 and 19, in proposing the recognition of achievement below the GCSE, and with those who have learning difficulties particularly in mind, it also extends to 14 to 16 year olds.

1.13 The Report makes proposals that are often capable of adoption in the next two to three years, so that an early response can be made to issues arising from the fast expansion of post-16 education and training. At the same time, the underpinning structure envisaged in the proposals is capable of further development and adaptation in the longer term, should that be appropriate.

Terms

1.14 It has been impossible to write this Report without constant reference to a host of qualifications and bodies of one kind or another, all with impressively long titles. To avoid the text being dominated by long recitals of names, extensive use of initials has been necessary. The reader is advised to refer to the list of abbreviations at Appendix 6.

1.15 To assist the reader four collective nouns have been used:

Government departments	Department for Education and Employment, the Welsh Office and the Northern Ireland Office
regulatory bodies	National Council for Vocational Qualifications (NCVQ); School Curriculum and Assessment Authority (SCAA); Curriculum and Assessment Authority for Wales (ACAC) and Council for the Curriculum, Examinations and Assessment (Northern Ireland) (CCEA), which set or approve national standards, and monitor the quality assurance and assessment arrangements of awarding bodies to ensure that they work fairly and effectively.
awarding bodies	The bodies which make awards such as the GCSE, A levels, the GNVQ and NVQ.
key skills	Skills in communication, the application of number and information technology.

2

Contents

SECTION 2

The background to decisions

The imperative to achievement

2.1   Education is about developing all the talents, abilities and faculties of young people. It is about developing them as human beings, and about preparing them for citizenship and parenthood as well as for the world of work. We should encourage all our young people to achieve as much as they are capable of, from those young people with serious learning difficulties, to those who are highly talented.

2.2   These are ends to which a nation should wish to aspire at any time. But the challenges of the next century bring the need for success into sharp focus. Education and training are central to the prospects of today's young people for earning a good standard of living.

2.3   This Report therefore recognises the need to achieve the National Targets for Education and Training shown in Table 1.

Table 1

(i)	By age 19, 85% of young people to achieve five **GCSEs** at grade **C** or above, an Intermediate **GNVQ** or a full **NVQ** level 2.
(ii)	75% of young people to achieve level 2 competence in communication, numeracy and information technology by age 19; and 35% to achieve level 3 competence in these skills by age 21.
(iii)	By age 21, 60% of young people to achieve 2 A levels, an Advanced **GNVQ** or a full **NVQ** level 3.

These targets, for the year 2000, have already been surpassed by Germany and Japan. The Report also recognises that in the future, relevant comparators will increasingly include the nations in the Far East, where the commitment to education in newly industrialised countries like Korea, Singapore and Taiwan is formidable. The need for high achievement will become increasingly evident as China, India and the Philippines, with working populations numbering some 900 million, progressively emerge as major economies, but with rates of earning a fraction of those in Britain. Economic development in parts of these nations is now advancing quickly, often in partnership with enterprises from the developed economies of the Far East and the West.

2.4   The only strategy for a nation seeking to maintain and enhance a high standard of living, lies in concentration on advanced products and services, a high level of innovation, challenging and constantly improving standards of achievement and competitiveness, based on a highly-educated, well-trained and adaptable workforce.

Priorities, values and life-long learning

2.5 The National Targets mean raising the present levels of achievement of large numbers of pupils in statutory schooling. They will also require a major increase in the proportion of the post-16 population engaged in full- and part-time education and training. In 1993/94, one in ten 16 year olds was not in education or training, a figure which was doubled at 17 and almost doubled again at 18.

2.6 Current   s follows.

Table 2

		1995 %	Targets for 2000 %	Increase needed (%)
Percentag an Interm		63	85	22
Percentag or full NV		44	60	16

2.7 The implication of these figures is clear. We must see today's under-achievers as an educational priority. The National Targets for Education and Training must be brought into our thinking at every level. The framework of qualifications should be instrumental in this.

2.8 In national terms, achievement in applied and vocational education ranks alongside the academic. Failure to recognise that is to do an immense disservice to today's young people. The nation needs to value good technicians and good graduates equally. A good share of our most able young people should choose to follow the applied and vocational pathways, confident that they are equally esteemed by society.

2.9 The need for learning to be life-long is now well-recognised and supported by National Targets for Lifetime Learning. Many of those now in schools and colleges will face the prospect of having to change careers several times in their working lives. Employers underline the speed at which change is taking place in industry, and the need for workers to be constantly adapting to new demands.

The spiritual and moral dimension of education

2.10 Education means preparing young people for life in the widest sense. As adults they will assume responsibility for the quality of our society and civilisation. Spiritual and moral values must therefore be an essential element in education. The Report raises the issue of how schools and colleges can build this dimension into their work and make it relevant to achievement in the various subject areas.

The institutions and the people

2.11 Although colleges of further education are often associated with adult education and training, they make a major contribution to the development of the young people with whom this Review is specifically concerned, covering the whole range of academic, applied and vocational qualifications.

2.12 In 1994, an analysis of the education and training of 17 year olds showed the following picture:

Table 3

17 Year Olds in:	%
Further education	32
School sixth forms	26
Government supported training	14
Employer–funded training	3
Other education and training	4
Not in education or training	21

2.13 This Report is concerned with all these young people, including those who are not in any form of education and training.

Teaching

2.14 Finally, and most importantly, the achievements in education and training to which we aspire, and the developments proposed in this Report, can only be realised through teachers, lecturers and trainers, and with their active support. My recommendations have important implications for the approach to learning and for teacher training and development; they assume that the potential of information and communications technology for enhancing the range, effectiveness and quality of teaching will continue to be harnessed. These issues will need particular attention in the action that follows this Report.

SECTION 3

Structures

A national framework of qualifications

3.1   The present range of qualifications, the complexity of the language surrounding them, the lack of a shared vocabulary of terms to describe them, and the pace of their development in recent years, means that those who are not closely involved with education and training are unable to grasp what is going on. The titles of most of the qualifications in our three main qualifications pathways for 16–19 year olds are distinctly unmemorable: General Certificate of Secondary Education (GCSE), General National Vocational Qualifications (GNVQs) and National Vocational Qualifications (NVQs). Only A levels are common currency with everyone.

3.2   For those whose achievements are below the level of these qualifications, there is no national provision for recognition.

3.3   Among those involved in education and training, whether as providers or learners, there is a strong wish for greater coherence in the framework of qualifications. Those outside want a framework they can understand. There is interest in a structure which makes it possible to combine elements from more than one pathway. There is a widely shared concern to lift the standing of the applied and vocational pathways, so that choices can more fully reflect young people's aptitudes and enthusiasms, and best respond to national needs. The historic pre-eminence of A levels has led to their expansion beyond the purposes for which they were created. Their further expansion would most probably serve to increase the already too high proportion of disappointed students who find the A level approach is not right for them.

3.4   A first step towards coherence is to bring the present academic, applied and vocational pathways into a common framework covering all achievements. A common framework would help people to understand where qualifications stand in relation to each other. Such a framework needs to recognise explicitly the equivalence in national terms of the value of achievement, whether through the A level and the GCSE, or through the GNVQ or the NVQ.

3.5   The common framework should also be capable of recognising other major qualifications currently available which meet nationally accepted criteria, but fall outside the three main qualifications pathways.

3.6   The recommendations that follow show how the main qualifications could be brought into a national framework, and illustrate the forms of the awards that would be made under it.

Recommendations

- A national framework for qualifications should be introduced to cover achievement in the three main pathways at four levels:

    - Advanced

    - Intermediate

    - Foundation

    - Entry

- They should be known as **National Levels,** and the term **National** should be used in front of all the main elements in the proposed framework[1]. These include:

    - National Awards

    - National Record of Achievement

    - National Traineeships

    - National Certificates

    - National Advanced Diploma

    - National Vocational Qualifications

- All certificates issued by awarding bodies should show the relevant national level prominently as the main heading. To assist understanding of what has been achieved, the new certificates should include (on the reverse side) a list of the main comparable, nationally recognised achievements at the relevant level. The face of the certificate should give more detail than at present about the nature of the achievement. For certificates at the Advanced level, provision should be made for including the numerical score based on the Universities and Colleges Admissions Service (UCAS) proposed new tariff. A certificate number should be included on each certificate.

- National criteria should be developed in order to recognise and formally ascribe national levels to other current major qualifications which fall outside the three main qualifications pathways.

- The grouping of present awards into four common national levels would be as shown in Table 4. The form of the new certificates would be as illustrated in Appendices 2, 3, 4 and 5. The equivalences of awards at the higher levels is based on those in the National Targets, though these are approximate and may need reassessment in the light of experience. The proposed national framework for awards makes plain that academic, applied and vocational qualifications at the same levels are of equal value.

---

[1] It should be for consideration to what extent in Wales these should be identified as 'Welsh National'.

7

3.7 The inclusion of an Entry level in this national framework of qualifications gives an opportunity to encourage and recognise achievement by a wider range of learners than at present. Proposals are contained in Section 7 for a new National Award at Entry level.

3.8 Section 6 of this Report also has a direct bearing on the framework: it contains recommendations on the size and structure of the Advanced GNVQ (Section 6.1-6.6) and on a reformulated AS qualification (Section 6.33-6.34).

Table 4 Proposed framework of national awards

National Award: Advanced Level

AS and A Level	GNVQ Advanced Level	NVQ Level 3†

National Award: Intermediate Level

GCSE Grades A*-C	GNVQ Intermediate Level	NVQ Level 2‡

National Award: Foundation Level

GCSE Grades D-G	GNVQ Foundation Level	NVQ Level 1‡

National Award: Entry Level*

Common to all pathways:
Three grades A/B/C

---

†   NVQ level 3 obtained by young people primarily through a Modern Apprenticeship/Employment.

‡   NVQ levels 1 and 2 obtained by young people primarily through Youth Training/Employment.

*   Entry Level at grades A, B, C equivalent in demand to Levels 3, 2 and 1 of the National Curriculum, but contextualised for the post-16 age group.

Clarity of purpose for the three main pathways

3.9 The GCSE, A level, GNVQ and NVQ qualifications have been developed to respond to distinctive needs. They offer much needed alternative approaches to learning, which are essential if all are to achieve their full potential. However, the positioning of each qualification needs continuing oversight by the regulatory bodies for two reasons:

- First, to ensure that the GNVQ, which was designed to be taught in schools and colleges to provide a broad education in terms of applying knowledge and understanding to the world of work, also provides an underpinning to the strictly vocational NVQ qualification. That twofold role means a proper balance must be maintained between these two purposes.

- Second, to prevent confusion in the minds of employers, universities and students about the distinctive roles of the A level and GCSE (on one side) and the GNVQ (on the other).

3.10 A later Section of the Report deals with the ways in which the GNVQ can support the NVQ. As to the interface between the "academic" qualifications and the more "applied" GNVQ, some broad distinguishing guidelines need to be set out. These would include differences in the purposes of the qualifications, in the subject areas appropriate to each pathway, and in the approaches to assessment.

Recommendations

- Drawing on broad principles outlined in the full Report (Section 3.22-3.25), a joint committee of the NCVQ and SCAA, with the involvement of Wales and Northern Ireland should enter into discussion with the awarding bodies and recommend broad principles for allocating subject areas to pathways, for the approval of the Secretaries of State.

- Below A level, it should be accepted that the GCSE develops general education as well as the practical application of skills, for example in communication and the application of number. But in subject areas outside the National Curriculum, or where GCSE subject-specific criteria do not already exist, studies in the practical applications of knowledge and understanding, relevant to broad areas of employment, should normally be regarded as the province of the GNVQ, unless there are good reasons to the contrary.

- The joint committee should consider all proposals for new awards and programmes, and make recommendations to the parent bodies. As qualifications come forward for revision and approval, their appropriateness for a particular pathway should be reviewed.

- The joint committee might also consider whether in the longer term there is a case for a national subject framework for qualifications based on coherent groupings of broad subject areas.

Transfer between pathways

3.11 Though the pathways should be distinct, A levels and GNVQs will often be taught in the same institutions, and some students may decide after embarking on a course that they have chosen the wrong pathway. In some areas an A level and a GNVQ include some common content. The Gatsby Foundation, in association with the Review, has undertaken a project to identify the extent of this commonality. Where it exists, this would enable a common core to be established, allowing students to change pathways after, say, the first term. Though the scope for this may be limited, it could be valuable in reducing wastage.

Recommendation

■ In the light of the outcome of the Gatsby project, awarding bodies should examine the scope for identifying common content in related areas of study in modular A levels and GNVQs, bearing in mind the feasibility of common elements being taught together, but without changing the distinctive nature and rigour of each of these qualifications.

Towards a common timetable and common arrangements for quality assurance

3.12 To support such developments, we need to bring greater coherence to the arrangements for quality assurance for qualifications within the national framework. These arrangements would include common timetables for the review, development and approval of qualifications in related subject areas. Such arrangements would need to recognise the distinctive characteristics of qualifications and avoid compromising them. But there is much to be gained from co-ordinating work across the binary line that divides our present arrangements.

Recommendation

■ The proposed joint committee of the NCVQ and SCAA, with the involvement of Wales and Northern Ireland, should develop a common timetable and common arrangements for quality assurance for all qualifications in the national framework.

The thickets of complexity and jargon

3.13 In addition to common arrangements for quality assurance, we need a shared vocabulary. The complex and specialist language of the qualifications framework and the lack of a common vocabulary of terms across awarding and regulatory bodies are a major barrier to public understanding.

Recommendation

■ Plain words and a common vocabulary should be adopted by the regulatory and the awarding bodies for all qualifications, as soon as is practicable.

The regulatory and awarding bodies

3.14 The arrangements for making awards and regulating them are currently divided by a binary line, with GCSE/A levels on one side and GNVQs and NVQs on the other. While some awarding bodies straddle this line, most do not. Arrangements in Wales and Northern Ireland are different from those in England, but similar issues arise.

3.15 The need to bridge this national divide in achievement and values was recognised by the widely-welcomed merger of the training and education functions of the Department for Education and Employment in England (DfEE).

3.16 The issue is how much further that process should be taken. During consultation, representations were made for the merger of the NCVQ and SCAA, and for a reduction in the number of awarding bodies. Closer working, or amalgamations, could achieve greater coherence in qualifications; effect a valuable transfer of experience and practice; help to avoid proliferation of courses and qualifications; and achieve a better understanding of the whole system of qualifications.

3.17 My Interim Report recommended that the NCVQ and SCAA should set up a joint committee to co-ordinate their work and identify the scope for a common approach to it. The Secretary of State invited Sir Michael Heron and me to put the recommendation into effect, and we have done so. At the same time several of the awarding bodies have been in discussions about mergers or closer associations, and one of each has taken place.

3.18 A momentum for change has now been created. This gives an opportunity to address the century-old division between education and training by introducing arrangements that span the divide.

Recommendations

- The Government Departments should encourage awarding bodies to come together across the binary line to create new joint arrangements for awarding the GCSE, A level and GNVQ.

- The Government Departments should, at the same time, take action to rationalise:

  - the number of bodies involved in the awarding of qualifications;

  - the number of NVQ awarding bodies.

- Legislation should be introduced to bring together the work of the NCVQ and SCAA.

- To that end the Government should consult on the following alternatives:

  - bringing together *all* the work of the NCVQ and SCAA into one single statutory body, *or*

☐ regrouping the qualifications and public examinations functions of the NCVQ and SCAA into a new National Qualifications Authority for England with a separate Authority responsible for the school curriculum from 4–19, for statutory assessment up to the age of 14, and possibly, in the interests of reducing the number of bodies involved in education, for some other functions.

■ The consultation should further consider how employment interests might best be represented in future arrangements to ensure that NVQs continue to be based on occupational standards and remain employment-led.

■ In the event of legislation, specific provision should be made for Wales and Northern Ireland.

■ In the meantime, the Government should support the co-ordinating work of the joint committee of the NCVQ and SCAA, with the full involvement of Wales and Northern Ireland.

SECTION 4

A restructuring and relaunch of two initiatives

4.1   Two existing initiatives for motivating and recognising achievement would benefit from new approaches; they are Youth Training and the National Record of Achievement (NRA). Modern Apprenticeships are also considered at the end of the Youth Training section, but there are no proposals for restructuring this initiative.

Youth Training

4.2   Nearly 280,000 young people are involved in Youth Training. The objective is that entrants should achieve an NVQ level 2. Its success in creating a well-skilled and adaptable community of workers of all kinds is fundamental to national competitiveness and to achieving the National Targets for Education and Training.

4.3   Though Youth Training offers a good work-based route to qualifications, its standing among young people is modest. Its status may suffer as Modern Apprenticeships attract many of the most able trainees. This problem of status needs to be tackled if the initiative is to succeed in doing the job for which it was created.

4.4   The Government guarantee of a training place to any young person not in full-time education or a job compounds the problem of standing. Some perceive Youth Training as being used by those who have little motivation to achieve, but wish to secure financial support from the state. The long-term prospects of young people in Youth Training are not helped by the absence of a requirement, as opposed to encouragement, to develop their skills in communication, the application of number and information technology, the key skills for adaptability in a rapidly changing world.

4.5   There are also some young people who are not yet ready for NVQ level 1. For these young people Entry level provision is necessary to help them develop their skills and prepare them for progression to NVQs and other qualifications.

4.6   Another concern is the completion rate. Whilst leaving a traineeship to take a job is wholly understandable, a completion rate of 46 per cent is unsatisfactory. Although in the period April 1994 to January 1995 half of the leavers obtained a full or part qualification, six months after leaving 22 per cent were known to be unemployed.

4.7   A new approach is needed.

Recommendations

■   Youth Training[1], however currently named, should be relaunched as a system of **National Traineeships,** available at **Foundation, Intermediate,** and perhaps **Advanced levels,** providing progression to Modern Apprenticeships and the work-based route.

---

[1]   Youth Training is known by a multiplicity of names in different TEC areas throughout the country.

■ **National Traineeships** should offer a broad and flexible learning programme for young people, designed by Industry Training Organisations and Training and Enterprise Councils (TECs), and delivered in partnership with colleges of further education. Each Traineeship should incorporate NVQs (at levels 1, 2 and perhaps 3 as appropriate to the industry), the three key skills of communication, the application of number and information technology, and (where appropriate) other units, short courses, and whole qualifications, such as GNVQs and GCSEs.

■ Acceptance to a National Traineeship should be based on an assessment of the applicant's suitability. It should not be the fall-back position for all young people without a job.

■ For those not yet ready for NVQ level 1, including those with special education and training needs and those unclear about their career direction, **National Entry level provision** should be developed, geared to the Entry level qualifications proposed in this Report (see Section 7). It should be available in a range of motivating vocational contexts and should encourage the development of key skills.

■ As with Modern Apprenticeships, applicants for National Traineeships and National Entry level provision should be required to enter into an agreement with the training provider/TEC, perhaps brokered by the Careers Service, which outlines the responsibilities of both the individual and the provider.

■ Clear routes of progression should be established so that young people can readily progress through the levels of the National Traineeship into Modern Apprenticeships, college-based provision or work as appropriate.

■ Quality assurance arrangements for National Traineeships should be developed consistent with those for the Modern Apprenticeship.

■ Appropriate arrangements should be devised for funding TECs to contribute with local partners to National Entry level provision.

■ Consideration should be given to reformulating the Government guarantee in the light of the development of the National Traineeship and National Entry level provision. Decisions on the appropriate Entry level for any individual should be based on a careful assessment of what is most appropriate for the individual applicant.

4.8   Ministers with responsibilities for Wales and Scotland will wish to consider how best to take these matters forward for their young people.

Modern Apprenticeships

4.9   This Government initiative was launched in 1995 and aims to attract able young people to develop their careers through the work-based route on a fast track to NVQ level 3. Subsequent options include proceeding to higher education, perhaps through a sandwich course, or continuing to develop a career through full-time employment. In consultation, employers have underlined their interest in attracting young people who would otherwise have chosen to take A levels, to enter work and develop their careers through this route. Similar initiatives have been a source of strength to competitor nations.

Recommendations

- Schools and the Careers Service should be well briefed so that young people have the Mod[...]m.

- Employe[...] not only the necessary skills, but suffic[...]ding to enable Modern Apprenti[...]on if they wish, to part-time, full-time, [...]d degrees.

- Progressi[...]r for young people who have attained [...]gress to Modern Apprentic[...]

- Employers [...] their deployment on the completio[...]omentum established is not lost.

- Participation and achievement for males and females, and people from minority ethnic groups, should be monitored at national, regional and industry sector levels.

The National Record of Achievement

4.10 The National Record of Achievement (NRA) was introduced in 1991 as an important vehicle for recording achievement and planning future learning. It has strong advocates in schools and colleges, but commitment to it varies. Many small- and medium-sized firms and employers have little knowledge of it. Students often have insufficient understanding of how to use it effectively in preparing a job application or at an interview. It has the potential to be much more than a summary of achievement. It could be an important instrument through which young people develop the practice of managing and taking responsibility for their own learning, as a skill they need for life, continuing through college, university and into work. The NRA links readily in the workplace to Investors in People. The NRA needs to be restructured and relaunched to achieve these purposes, and, as reformulated, to receive the support of employers. That employer support is essential to provide the motivation for the associated work in schools and colleges, which will pay dividends to them.

Recommendations

- The NRA should be reviewed and relaunched.

- The NRA should have a major role in developing skills in planning and managing one's own learning through a self-contained section which guides the learner through the process. In colleges, the use of 'learning agreements', through which students set targets for their own learning, will support the development of these skills, and contribute directly to the restructured NRA.

- During 16–19 education and training, consideration should be given to assessing and certificating young people's skills in planning and managing their own learning. This could be done through the NCVQ's unit, 'improving own learning and performance'. Although formal assessment of these skills should be optional, recognition of the award of the NCVQ unit should be given in the Universities and Colleges Admissions Service (UCAS) proposed new profile and tariff.

■ The NRA should be introduced to pupils when judgements are being made about the last two years of statutory schooling, say at 13$\frac{1}{2}$ years. The present quality folder provided by the Government should be available to all pupils at that age.

■ Use of the NRA throughout lifetime learning should be strongly encouraged and supported by the Government, Local Education Authorities (LEAs), employers, TECs, schools, colleges, universities and other institutions.

■ Use of the NRA as a tool for lifetime learning should be encouraged through Investors in People.

■ All students should receive guidance from schools and colleges on using the NRA in applying for a university place, or a job, and in interviews.

■ The existing 'Qualifications and Credits' sheet in the NRA should be retitled 'Record of National Awards' and used to record all qualifications and units at national level.

■ Consideration should be given to making the NRA processes of recording achievement and action planning part of the schools' and colleges' inspection frameworks.

S E C T I O N 5

National targets and needs: new initiatives

Improving skills for work and life-time learning

5.1 There is much concern in all quarters about current standards of achievement in communication and the application of number, including mental arithmetic, and the ability to estimate. No other issues attracted more comment during the Review from employers and higher education.

5.2 In English (Welsh), this concern applied to the written language and especially to oracy. For recruits at 18 and 21, employers are looking for a high level of skill in oral communication, including the ability to make effective presentations and respond to questions. They feel entitled to look to school and college education to provide this.

5.3 Employers recognise the growing importance of competence in the use of information technology as a life-time skill.

5.4 In addition, they value certain general skills which the GNVQ is intended to develop, and look for the development of similar skills among A level and graduate entrants. These include:

- Skills in working effectively with other people.

- Presentational skills.

- A problem-solving approach.

- The ability to manage one's own learning as a necessity in a society that needs to be committed to life-long learning.

5.5 Employers and universities are interested in applicants' experience, achievement and commitments beyond their main studies. These are seen as contributing to the development of the skills listed above, broadening a young person's understanding of society in general, and developing personal qualities.

Developing key skills

5.6 Prime responsibility for developing the three key skills, in communication, the application of number and information technology lies with schools, during compulsory schooling from 5–16. The recent revision of the National Curriculum was intended to give schools more opportunity to devote time to develop these skills. While this Review has been proceeding, SCAA and ACAC have made proposals to the Government designed to achieve higher standards in English, Welsh and mathematics. But employers and universities are concerned to see these key skills, and competence in the use of information technology, continuing to develop after 16, with students accumulating experience in applying them in a range of contexts. Employers have urged the need for a response to their concerns.

Recommendations

GCSE

■ To underline the importance of number, the regulatory and awarding bodies should provide a separate grading for those aspects of GCSE mathematics concerned with calculation, estimation, and statistics which would be shown separately on the face of the certificate. This would complement the recent proposal by the Secretaries of State to give a separate grading for spoken English and Welsh alongside the overall grade for the GCSE in these subjects.

■ In information technology (for which a range of full, combined-subject or short course GCSEs and other vocational qualifications already exist, but none of which is necessarily taken by all students) the NCVQ units in information technology should be approved as a basis for assessment at Key Stage 4 in schools. Schools should be encouraged to offer appropriate information technology qualifications to all pupils.

A Levels

■ The A level subject cores and syllabuses should be reviewed by the appropriate regulatory and awarding bodies to identify what further scope there is to build in relevant elements in communication, the application of number and information technology without distorting the integrity of individual subjects.

■ A new 'AS in key skills', recognising attainment in communication, the application of number and information technology, should be created by the regulatory bodies. This should be developed alongside a review of the present requirements in these three key skills for the Advanced level GNVQ. But whilst the GNVQ provides a minimum requirement to support the main area of study, the new AS would be a separate graded award which builds on the skills developed pre-16. Assessment would be based on course work and examination. Skills would be demonstrated in a context relevant to the main areas of study, and students would be required to achieve a minimum level of achievement in each skill for an overall award. Students should be strongly advised to acquire this AS, which should attract a numerical score in the proposed new UCAS profile and tariff.

GNVQs

■ The present GNVQ requirements in communication, the application of number and information technology at level 3 should be reviewed alongside the consideration of the new AS in key skills.

■ NCVQ should consider the introduction of simple-to-use tests to contribute to the assessment of the mandatory units in communication, the application of number and information technology.

NVQs

■ All young people on NVQ programmes funded at public expense should be required to take advantage of the facilities offered for developing the three key skills, but the award of the NVQ should not be dependent on achievement of units beyond those mandatorily required for the NVQ.

■ Lead bodies should review closely the extent to which key skills are directly relevant to the competence attested by an award, and ensure that they are built into their requirements at each level.

General recommendations on the three key skills

■ All schools, colleges and training bodies providing education and training for 16–19 year olds which is publicly funded, should provide opportunities for all young people to develop their key skills and to have them assessed and recognised.

■ The award of the proposed National Certificates and Diploma (see Section 5.7-5.20) should be dependent upon achievement of the three key skills at the appropriate level.

■ Universities and employers should be urged to make a particular point of looking for and making clear to applicants for places that the possession of the new AS in key skills or the NCVQ equivalent will bear on their decisions on recruitment.

■ Teachers will need help and guidance through programmes of staff development, to enable them to provide opportunities for the further development of key skills within A level courses, and to prepare them for teaching the new AS in key skills.

Personal and inter-personal skills

■ All learners, including A level students, should be given opportunities by institutions to practise making oral presentations to peer groups, to engage in discussion on their presentations, and to tackle projects through group work to develop their experience of team-working.

■ Learners should be encouraged to record their achievements in these skills in their National Record of Achievement and to gain certification through NCVQ units in 'improving own learning and performance' and 'working with others' post-16.

■ Institutions should be encouraged to identify opportunities for developing learners' personal and inter-personal skills in their development plans, and this should be monitored by inspection bodies.

The National Targets and National Certificates

5.7 The three main issues emerging from this Review are:

■ The need to achieve the National Targets for Education and Training for the year 2000.

■ The need to make a determined national effort to raise standards in communication and the application of number, and to build competence in the use of information technology.

■ The need to bring coherence to the national framework of qualifications, to help understanding of them, to increase opportunity, and to recognise the equal national regard for qualifications, whether they be academic, applied or vocational.

5.8 If the national targets are to be achieved, and if standards in the three key skills are to be raised, they need to be at the centre of national attention. The targets must be owned by those who are in a position, at all levels, to influence their achievement. Training and Enterprise Councils (TECs), Local Education Authorities (LEAs) and other relevant partners are involved in setting local targets through strategic forums. TECs are contractually obliged to report annually on progress against these targets, and the DfEE is currently developing a synthesis of this information. The Government has also recognised the role of Industry Training Organisations in setting targets for industry sectors.

5.9 However, there is a concern about the lack of consistency on how baseline information is calculated, how targets are set and how progress is measured. There is also variation in the extent of the involvement of individual schools and colleges in the process of local target setting. This needs to be put right so that there is an effective chain from national to local level for the achievement of the targets, and action should be taken to that effect.

5.10 In addition, to put the targets in clear focus at the level of the school and college and in the minds of young people, and to assist measurement of achievement against them, a National Certificate should be introduced to recognise achievement equal to, or greater than, National Target levels of attainment. It should be issued on the authority of the teaching institutions, where the young person is attached to one, or by a TEC, when it is earned in the workplace. The underlying authority for this National Certificate would be the certificates issued by the National Awarding Bodies. The National Certificate would recognise both achievement built up over time and combinations of achievement across the three pathways that comply with the national standards.

5.11 As the present National Targets do not provide an explicit link between achievement in the main qualifications and achievement in the three key skills of communication, the application of number and information technology, these two aspects should be brought together to define the requirement for the award of the National Certificate.

Recommendations

5.12 A National Certificate should be introduced to recognise achievement at the Intermediate and Advanced levels. The requirements should be as follows.

- **Intermediate level:** a minimum of five GCSEs at grade C or above, including English/Welsh, mathematics, and the full, combined-subject or short course GCSE in information technology[1]; or a GNVQ at Intermediate level, or full NVQ at level 2. Where GCSEs in English/Welsh, mathematics and information technology have not been achieved at grade C or above, competence must be demonstrated in the NCVQ units of communication, the application of number and information technology at level 2.

- **Advanced level:** two A level passes, or a full GNVQ at Advanced level, or a full NVQ at level 3, plus competence in communication, the application of number and information technology demonstrated through the NCVQ units at level 3, or through the proposed new AS in key skills, these being harmonised to be of the same standard (see Section 5.6).

- Consideration should be given to the creation of a National Certificate at the Foundation level.

---

[1] Due allowance could be made for particular requirements in Wales, such as the possible inclusion of science.

- Work should be carried out to identify those major awards, other than A levels, GCSEs, GNVQs and NVQs, which should count for recognition towards the achievement of the National Certificate at the Intermediate and Advanced levels.

- The National Certificate should be designed to recognise achievement over and above the minimum requirements for the award.

- The Government should work with LEAs , TECs and other relevant partners to ensure that the setting, monitoring and achievement of local targets is consistent with and contributes to the National Targets for Education and Training.

- In addition, LEAs, TECs and the Further Education Funding Councils should work with locally managed and grant maintained schools and colleges on setting, monitoring and achieving institutional targets, linked to the National Certificates.

- The Government should consider the case for governing bodies of schools and colleges to report on progress against institutional targets as part of the annual report to parents and the wider community.

- The National Certificate should be issued by schools and colleges, and for those at work, by TECs, on the basis of awards made by the awarding bodies, with strong arrangements to ensure tight control over the granting of certificates and safeguards against fraudulent practice.

A National Diploma at the Advanced level: to encourage studies in depth, with complementary studies to give breadth

5.13 For at least forty years there has been debate on whether England, Wales and Northern Ireland are right to adopt a policy of specialisation in post-16 education, or whether it would be better to adopt the policy widely practised in other parts of the Western world, and to a degree in Scotland, of broadly-based studies.

5.14 In 1959, the Crowther Committee concluded that the pursuit of two or three A levels was the best educational option for A level students, with some additional breadth coming through common and complementary studies. A succession of reviews since then has recommended a move to greater breadth, usually involving the study of a broader range of subjects.

5.15 Most recently the National Commission on Education made proposals which, at the Advanced level, would involve in-depth study of a major programme area, and balancing studies in three other programme areas forming between a third and a half of the total programme. The Commission also proposed a requirement to cover core skills.

5.16 In its 1991 White Paper on *Education and Training for the 21st Century*, the Government noted that the specialised study of two or three subjects, often closely related to each other, is for many students too narrow a preparation for the next stage of study or work.

5.17 In consultation during the present Review, there has been much support from teaching institutions for a reformulated AS to encourage broader studies. But the whole institutional framework in schools, colleges and universities is based on progressive specialisation. There is also concern that any change would undermine the standard of A levels.

5.18 Since the 1950s, when less than 5 per cent of the age group went on to university, we have moved into mass post-16 education and training. Leading commentators argue that the pace of change is now such that most people who are in education today will have to change careers more than once. They would be helped by an education that equips them to do that.

5.19 This Report is based on the premise that the foundation of education and training policy should be diversity and choice. This leads to the conclusion that young people should have a wide range of choices at 16. One option should be to combine study in depth with complementary studies to give breadth. To enable such an option to get off the ground, it needs special recognition within the family of national certificates, and a level of achievement that will command the respect of universities.

Recommendations

■ A distinctive diploma at Advanced level should be created to recognise achievement in studies both in depth and in breadth, to be known as the National Advanced Diploma ('The Diploma').

■ The heart of this award would be two full A levels, *or* a full Advanced GNVQ, *or* a full NVQ at level 3, *or* agreed equivalents.

■ Breadth would be provided by studies in complementary areas so that between the studies in depth and those in breadth, four broadly defined areas of study would be covered to the minimum of the new AS proposed in Section 6.33-34. For A level students, these areas might be defined as:

  □ science, technology, engineering and mathematics;

  □ modern languages (including Welsh for students for whom it is not their first language);

  □ the arts and humanities (including English and Welsh); and

  □ the way the community works (including business, economics, government and politics, law, psychology and sociology).

■ For the GNVQ and NVQ a complementary approach would be needed, based on coherent groupings of units from subject areas other than the main study, which would include a modern language.

■ Studies in supporting areas would need to be at least an AS qualification, or the equivalent, in terms of units from the GNVQ or NVQ.

■ In addition, all those seeking this diploma would need to achieve standards in the three key skills through either the proposed AS in key skills or the NCVQ units in communication, the application of number and information technology at level 3, these being harmonised to be of the same standard.

5.20 These would be the *minimum* requirements. The new diploma should also recognise achievement above the minimum.

S E C T I O N   6

National qualifications

General National Vocational Qualifications (GNVQs)

6.1 The form of learning associated with the GNVQ is proving highly motivating to a large number of students. Though it was designed for students after the age of 16, there is a growing take-up among 14–16 year olds. In 1994–95 an estimated 130,000 16–18 year olds were pursuing GNVQ Advanced or Intermediate courses in schools and colleges. That number was a considerable increase on 1993–94. It is expected to continue to increase rapidly as more young people opt for GNVQs post-16 as the range of the GNVQ programme increases.

6.2 The rapid growth of the GNVQ has entailed some substantial problems. In particular, there is concern about the sheer burden of assessment and about its rigour. The Committee chaired by Dr John Capey made recommendations to address these problems, and I welcome its conclusions.

6.3 It is fundamental to this Review that the GNVQ should retain its present purposes and distinctive characteristics, and continue to increase its take-up. But there are issues relating to its structure and name that need attention.

6.4 The GNVQ was designed as a grouped award, being broadly equivalent in weight at the Foundation and Intermediate levels to four GCSEs, and at the Advanced level to two A levels. The size of the full award creates some problems.

6.5 A large grouped award like the GNVQ increases the risk of non-completion. Only half those who began a GNVQ programme in 1993 had achieved a full award after two years. The Advanced GNVQ is too big to be taken by students who choose A level as their main route, but who would benefit from some work in a GNVQ.

6.6 There is also the issue of the name. The GNVQ as a name is hardly memorable, and the qualification is not, strictly speaking, vocational. It does not provide training for a trade or profession, but rather education in the application of knowledge and understanding to a broad area of industrial or commercial life, and the development of general skills valued in the workplace. While teachers and students are becoming increasingly aware of the GNVQ, and while those involved rightly have pride in their achievements, it is all too evident that a new qualification takes many years to achieve recognition. The Government recognised this and proposed to rename the GNVQ 'Vocational A levels'. In the consultations leading to this Report, 'Applied A levels' was considered a better title.

Recommendations

- The title 'Applied A level' should replace GNVQ (Advanced level), and this term should be adopted on all awarding certificates.

- Because of the size of the full GNVQ and the desirability of building up a common structure with A level, the Advanced GNVQ should be structured and named as follows:

Full GNVQ of 12 units, plus the three NCVQ units in communication, the application of number and information technology	Applied A level (Double Award)
Six units plus the three NCVQ units in communication, the application of number and information technology	Applied A level

- Detailed consideration should be given to the creation of a three unit award at Advanced level to be known as the Applied AS, to match the AS in the A level family, so that the GNVQ family would be completed by:

Three prescribed mandatory units	Applied AS

- Further consultation should be undertaken to establish whether the GNVQs at Intermediate and Foundation levels, and Part One GNVQs, should be renamed. Proposals for consultation could include the names 'Applied Intermediate levels' and 'Applied Foundation levels'.

6.7 Business and industry representatives have expressed concern that the GNVQ is not adequately supporting the NVQ. There is also a need to ensure that GNVQs prepare young people for the demands that will be made on them in higher education. With only 15 GNVQs planned, and 800 NVQs in existence, there is an obvious problem. The NCVQ has already responded with additional and optional units, but these need to be greatly increased. The NCVQ should be able to look with confidence to the lead bodies that develop NVQ standards to provide the basis for them. The development of additional GNVQ units, based on the knowledge and understanding required for the NVQ, will provide a valuable bridge between GNVQ and NVQ provision, and a means of specifying the knowledge and understanding underpinning the NVQs.

Recommendation

- Additional units should be developed to extend the choice of units available to GNVQ students so that they and others can direct their studies more closely to particular NVQs and build up the required knowledge and understanding underpinning them.

- There should be close and continuing monitoring of the experience of universities, and of students who have gained places on the basis of the GNVQ.

6.8 At the Entry level to the National Framework of Qualifications (see Section 7) there is a need for young people who are motivated in that direction to have access to applied learning which can receive recognition as proposed in this Report.

Recommendation

- The regulatory and awarding bodies should develop units and qualifications which provide opportunities for applied learning at the proposed Entry level and progression to Foundation level.

National Vocational Qualifications (NVQs)

6.9 The NVQ relies for its rationale and success on its integration into industry and commerce and on effective control being exercised by line managers. Recognising that each NVQ should reflect the particular needs of each branch of industry for which it was designed, no proposals are made in this Report to bring the structure of the NVQ into line with other qualifications. In turn, employers need to act decisively on their own perceptions of the complexity of the NVQ, its jargon, and the large number of awarding bodies. Line managers must take the opportunities through appropriate bodies to improve the clarity and relevance of NVQs following the lead given by the Beaumont Review.

6.10 The number of bodies accredited to award NVQs is causing problems. In contrast to A levels, NVQs are identical whoever administers them, although there are concerns that the quality and standards of assessment vary to an unacceptable extent, and it is often argued that fewer bodies should be involved.

Recommendation

■ As proposed in the Beaumont report, partnerships between awarding bodies and cross-recognition of centre approvals and procedures should be strengthened. The NCVQ and the DfEE should work with awarding bodies to secure rational and coherent provision, in the interests of customers of the system.

6.11 There have been concerns that the expression of NVQs, and the assessment of them, in terms of the required competences has been at the expense of building up the underpinning knowledge and understanding. The development of additional GNVQ units which specify this has been recommended above (see Section 6.7).

6.12 Another issue arising from consultation is whether those following an NVQ should be required to develop their skills in communication, the application of number and information technology and demonstrate this through the special NCVQ units in them. This is particularly relevant for young people. Earlier recommendations (Section 4) aim to make provision for this in relation to Youth Training and the Modern Apprenticeship. But young people should not be denied an NVQ simply because they have not achieved a given level of key skills, unless that is required for the NVQ itself. Employers should consider very carefully the adequacy of the existing requirements for the key skills in their NVQs.

Recommendation

■ Those designing NVQs should consider carefully what level of competence in the three key skills is appropriate for people to be considered professionally qualified at all levels, and build these requirements into each NVQ. At level 3 and above in particular, employers should encourage all young people to acquire the free-standing NCVQ units in the three key skills.

Rigour in GNVQs and NVQs

6.13 As well as its manageability, assessment in the GNVQ and in the NVQ have caused concern. The NCVQ has already taken action to improve the rigour of both qualifications – that is, assessment which is clear, fit for its purpose, and delivering valid and reliable outcomes. The issue is addressed in the reports by Mr Beaumont and Dr Capey. I welcome their recommendations, and recognise the need to ensure that any changes lead to simpler, more manageable, reliable and cost-effective assessment.

6.14 In particular, I welcome for the GNVQ:

- the proposal that assessment should be based on an overall assessment of performance in the units of which the qualification is built up, rather than on performance in all the individual elements which make up each unit;

- proposals for basing grading criteria on the two themes of 'process' and 'quality of outcomes';

- greater use of external assessment to help reduce the overall burden of internal assessment and to give assurance of uniform standards;

- the use of externally set assignments to contribute towards grading;

- an examination of the feasibility of using externally set and moderated standard assignments in a vocational context for the three key skills;

- a review of the role of external tests, in particular to:

  - reconsider whether candidates should be required to answer questions covering the entire range of knowledge specified in a mandatory unit;

  - consider whether the tests should be graded and, if so, the basis of grading;

  - take account of what has been learned from the use of extension tests and controlled assignments in the Part One GNVQs.

- external tests common to the three awarding bodies which I **recommend** should be given urgent consideration and be approved in advance by NCVQ.

- the provision of a specification of the required knowledge and understanding for the GNVQ, where this would be helpful.

6.15 Beyond that there will be wider lessons to be learnt from the Part One GNVQ pilots, and I welcome the intention of the regulatory bodies to work together and to monitor developments closely.

6.16 In relation to the NVQ, the Beaumont Committee also found a need to improve assessment and to reduce its costs, stressing that there 'must be an overriding requirement to demonstrate rigour'. While this could include external assessment, a combination of methods will be required which will vary between different qualifications and levels. An assessment model is to be developed, to provide guidance on the selection of assessment methods, which will be used by the NCVQ and the Scottish Vocational Education Council (responsible for Scottish Vocational Qualifications, the equivalent to NVQs in Scotland) to accredit qualifications.

6.17 I welcome these proposals to improve the quality of assessment of the NVQ and its verification, and the search for greater cost-effectiveness. External verification, and the training of external verifiers, is particularly important in ensuring rigorous assessment coupled with greater clarity in the statements of what is required of candidates to justify an award.

National data on GNVQs and NVQs

6.18 Changes are being made at a national level to improve the quality of data available on GNVQs and NVQs. I welcome these changes which, when implemented, should provide reliable information about take-up, wastage, and completions, and contribute to judgements about the rigour of these qualifications.

Other vocational qualifications

6.19 Coherence is needed in vocational qualifications. Outside the GNVQ and the NVQ, colleges provide a wide range of vocational qualifications for which there is proven demand. The intention has been that these should be absorbed into the GNVQ and the NVQ, in the interests of coherence and nation-wide standards. That in principle is right, and the policy should be pursued, but even where GNVQs and NVQs have been introduced, existing qualifications such as the BTEC Nationals are still being taken in colleges of further education.

6.20 There are legitimate claims that some of the existing qualifications cater for needs that are not met either by an NVQ that requires the candidate to have access to relevant employment, or by the broadly-based GNVQ. With the recommendations from the Beaumont review for a 'pre-NVQ' based on knowledge and skills rather than full competence in an occupation, the time is ripe for drawing these other qualifications into a more coherent framework that better meets the needs of candidates and employers. Precisely how this is to be achieved is still to be determined, but I would expect many of these existing qualifications to be mapped on to NVQs and GNVQs to make clear to users how they fit with NVQ assessment and how they could add to GNVQs.

6.21 I **recommend** that the NCVQ, in conjunction with the vocational awarding bodies, should pursue the following proposals for increasing coherence in the field of school and college-based vocational training:

■ Map existing qualifications for which there is substantial demand on to GNVQs and NVQs to identify areas of overlap or close relationship.

■ Increase the pool of optional and additional units in GNVQs to allow for greater specialisation.

■ Consider greater flexibility in the structure of GNVQs, for example by reducing the number of mandatory units required in those awards without compromising comparability.

■ Take into account the implications of the proposal for six unit awards based on the full GNVQ at Advanced level outlined in Section 6.6.

■ Consider the need for full GNVQs in new areas.

■ Look for ways of certificating existing qualifications as part of an NVQ or GNVQ.

6.22 Nevertheless a range of awards will continue outside this framework, often in response to the desire for locally customised provision which meets the requirements of particular groups of learners or employees. Much of this provision is accredited through the Open College Networks (OCNs) which provide a thorough quality assurance system and progression routes to national awards.

Recommendation

■ Links should be developed between the regulatory bodies and the National Open College Network to ensure that OCN accreditation leads to complementary local provision rather than a replication of national awards.

A levels

6.23 The demand for A levels is great. They have high standing with students, parents, employers and higher education. I was invited in undertaking the Review to maintain their rigour and to ensure that standards are being upheld.

6.24 There have been questions whether all A levels in all subjects are equally demanding, and also whether equal standards are required by all awarding bodies across the wide range of syllabuses and options available in many subjects. There has been concern whether the level of demand has been maintained over time and also about the possible impact on standards of the rapid take-up of modular A levels. There have been calls to make the required outcomes more explicit as with the vocational qualifications.

6.25 An independent study, and another by SCAA using the same methodology, suggests that the demands made in some subjects at A level are greater than in others. This applies to a group of subjects which includes mathematics, physics, chemistry and some modern foreign languages. Assuming these results are valid, there can be no levelling down in standards. University departments are already concerned about the adequacy of existing requirements in mathematics and some sciences.

6.26 Turning to the question of whether the same standards are required by the different awarding bodies, there are problems for the regulatory bodies in ensuring that common standards are maintained. The sheer number of alternative syllabuses that are available in popular subjects, and in some subjects the extensive range of options within a syllabus, makes close comparisons difficult. A further factor in the situation is the practice of schools and colleges from time to time making a change in the awarding body they use in a particular subject. Such a change may be made for valid reasons – for example, to offer a syllabus which is better suited to particular teaching methods. Almost inevitably, however, changing syllabuses sometimes raises the question whether schools or colleges hope that their candidates will achieve higher grades on the new syllabus.

6.27 Concern over the possibility that standards have diminished over time centres on the fact that there has been a small continuing annual rise in the average grade achieved in recent years, in spite of the progressive rise in the percentage of the age group taking

A levels (now over 30 per cent). Studies in England being undertaken by SCAA, jointly with the Office for Standards in Education, to examine these concerns in examinations at 16+ and 18+, have been handicapped by the limited archive material available, and comparisons are made difficult by the way the content of subjects has changed. I had hoped that the results of these studies would be available for this Report, but it will take some time to reach reliable conclusions. One of the three subjects covered by the studies is mathematics and I am able to comment on standards in mathematics in the light of the wider consultation underpinning this Review (see Section 6.31-6.32).

6.28 In modular A levels the ability to resit individual modules, and the spreading of assessment over time, gives some potential for higher achievement than in the traditional linear A level, where so much depends on the final examination. It is possible that this, and the popularity of the modular approach, could lead to the traditional A levels, which have established a high reputation over the years, being largely superseded. That raises two issues: first the need to be satisfied that the modular A level maintains a high level of demand, and second, whilst recognising the strong arguments made for modular A levels, to what extent it would be desirable to lose the kind of challenge that the traditional linear A level has represented. That in turn suggests that if it seemed likely that the modular A level would largely supersede the traditional A level, a format should be developed that incorporated the strength of both approaches.

6.29 The rapid increase in the take-up of modular A levels has also raised management issues for schools and colleges arising from the different patterns of examination sessions of the different awarding bodies. Some institutions are concerned about the increasing complexity of examination schedules and would prefer a degree of standardisation in module examination timetables.

6.30 I have no doubt about the integrity of the awarding bodies or of their concerns to maintain standards. The standing which A levels have achieved over 45 years reflects their success in this. But with the demands made upon the system by the wide range of syllabuses, together with the rapid take-up of modular A levels, present arrangements need reinforcing to ensure that standards are maintained across awarding bodies, between subjects and over time.

Recommendations

■ There should be no reduction in the required standard in any A level subject. The regulatory and awarding bodies should review the validity of the evidence in the main Report indicating differing standards between subjects, and in the light of their conclusions, raise the demand of any subjects found to be decidedly below the average to match the typical level of demand. Details of the procedure for bringing about this change should be agreed between the regulatory and awarding bodies, and be subject to approval by the Secretaries of State.

■ Each school and college should have a formal procedure, involving the head/ principal of the institution, before a decision is taken to change an awarding body.

■ The regulatory bodies, working in partnership with the awarding bodies, should reduce the number of syllabuses and options to levels where it is practical for them to be satisfied that equal standards prevail without requiring an unreasonable level of resources for the task, while preserving a reasonable choice for centres.

■ To strengthen the powers of the regulatory bodies which at present rely on informal arrangements, the Secretaries of State should consider implementing Section 24 of the Education Reform Act. (See Section 10 of the full Report.)

■ The awarding bodies should maintain a comprehensive archive of examination papers, scripts, mark schemes, coursework examination statistics and awards so that there is a better basis to assess standards over time. The form and extent of this archive should be agreed between the Government Departments, regulatory and awarding bodies.

■ Similar archives for checking standards over time should be set up for GNVQs, taking into account their distinctive characteristics and what it would be feasible to retain, and the effects on schools and colleges. The basis of this archive should be agreed between the Government Departments, the awarding bodies and the NCVQ.

■ In addition to the annual checks of standards, the regulatory bodies (in association with the awarding bodies) should undertake an in-depth review of standards, so that over five years all subjects are covered, to ensure that standards are being maintained over time and across awarding bodies.

■ The regulatory bodies should monitor closely the comparability and consistency of standards in modular and traditional linear A levels, and publish an annual report on this.

■ Both linear and modular A levels should be retained but:

  □ the final examination in a modular scheme of assessment should count for not less than 30 per cent of the total marks, and should test understanding of the syllabus as a whole;

  □ there should be a limit on the number of resits of any one module, to be determined by the regulatory bodies after consultation with the awarding bodies;

  □ there should be a common timetable for modular examinations, based on two sittings a year, probably in January and June. The joint committee of NCVQ and SCAA, with the involvement of Wales and Northern Ireland, should consider this issue in consultation with the awarding bodies, considering at the same time the timing of GNVQ tests.

■ As a possible policy for the longer term consideration should be given to combining the traditional and modular A levels into a unified approach. This might typically involve a structure of three modules accounting for the first half of the syllabus, and a final examination covering the remaining half, which would also include questions that test understanding of the syllabus as a whole.

■ The regulatory bodies should examine the extent to which it is practical and advantageous to take further the specification of A levels in terms of required outcomes, and whether it is possible to maintain a fresh stream of questions for modular examinations.

Mathematics and the sciences at A level

6.31 There are concerns about the declining proportion of students choosing to specialise in mathematics and the sciences; about standards, especially in mathematics at A level; and about the range of syllabuses, which means that universities have to begin teaching at a lower level than if students had followed a more common syllabus.

6.32 The concerns about the requirements for A level mathematics have been expressed particularly strongly, with the comment that a four year degree course may be required unless the present situation can be improved. In the consultations, particular reference has been made to the need in A levels for more algebra, and concerns have been expressed about limited perceptions of precision and proof, a declining ability to handle multi-step problems, and a lack of facility with number. All this bears on the preparedness of students for courses in chemistry, physics and engineering, as well as of those preparing to read mathematics at university.

Recommendations

Mathematics

- Schools and colleges should encourage students proposing to take A level mathematics to take a GCSE paper in additional mathematics, whether equivalent in weight to a GCSE short course or a full GCSE.

- The regulatory bodies should encourage awarding bodies to seek approval under Section 5 of the Education Act 1988, so that the existing certificates in mathematics can form a new, challenging GCSE course in additional mathematics, limited to grades A*-C.

- The regulatory bodies should review the range of curriculum material available to support courses to bridge the gap between GCSE and A level and, if necessary, stimulate the development of additional materials.

- The regulatory bodies, noting the concerns expressed in consultation about inadequate coverage of important areas of mathematics, drawing on the advice of the consultation group established by SCAA and the results obtained in due course from the study of standards over time, should enter into discussion with the awarding bodies about the requirements for A level mathematics, including the size of the mandatory core.

- Schools and colleges should encourage students to make more use of further mathematics courses through which students can supplement the main A level course. If double mathematics is not practicable, a further mathematics course equal in weight to the AS would be of benefit.

- The regulatory bodies should enter into discussions with the awarding bodies to maintain a good range of options while reducing overlapping provision.

- The regulatory bodies should investigate the feasibility of devising A level mathematics courses targeted at specific levels of attainment, or containing content designed for specific purposes.

The sciences

- The regulatory bodies should collect evidence to establish whether the current range of GCSE courses in the sciences satisfactorily provides both broad science education and sufficient preparation for further study at A level, and report their conclusions to the Secretaries of State.

- Schools should use 20 per cent of curriculum time for double science, as urged by the Royal Society.

- The regulatory bodies should enter into discussions with the awarding bodies with a view to increasing the size of the A level subject core in the sciences and reducing the number of syllabuses currently available, while maintaining some scope for a range of syllabuses.

- Awarding bodies should note the comments that some of the more demanding content of syllabuses does not feature sufficiently in examinations.

- SCAA should assess the provision for chemistry in the light of the outcome of the study of standards over time.

Improving the take-up of mathematics and the sciences

- Building upon the work of the Teacher Training Agency (TTA), the regulatory bodies should develop a programme of further research into factors affecting the attitudes of parents, pupils and teachers to mathematics and the sciences.

- The regulatory bodies and the TTA should identify and disseminate measures arising from this research to encourage a greater take-up of mathematics and the sciences.

- Interactive learning packages of high quality designed for use in schools and colleges merit the kind of development that has been taking place in universities.

- SCAA's mathematics and science consultative group should explore further the issues considered in this Section of the Report, with a view to some early decisions and action, and guide SCAA in further research and policy development. ACAC and CCEA should consider parallel action in Wales and Northern Ireland respectively.

- The NCVQ should continue to keep in consultation with universities and employers to monitor the progress of the Science GNVQ closely, so that its quality and fitness for purpose are assured, with a view to the GNVQ at Advanced level providing an additional source of scientists and science technicians.

A reformulated AS

6.33 The present AS was introduced to encourage students to pursue a broader range of studies. It has not succeeded in achieving its objective. But greater breadth of study post-16 is still desirable. A reformulated AS would aim to secure that objective and also offers a realistic goal for those who, having started an A level course, conclude that successful completion of it is beyond their reach. In this it will help to reduce wastage.

6.34 This points to reformulating the AS so that it covers the first half of the A level syllabus and represents the level of achievement expected after one full year's Advanced level study. This would allow it to be timetabled with the A level and help to ensure viable teaching groups.

Recommendations

- The reformulated AS should replace the existing AS and should represent the first half of the A level syllabus so that the two can be taught together.

- The existing AS and A subject cores should be reviewed and, where necessary, revised to ensure that the reformulated AS builds from and extends the content and level of demand of the GCSE. The AS core should cover those aspects of the A level most relevant to young people who may not wish to progress to the full award, as well as providing a firm foundation for progression to the full A level.

- The reformulated AS should be called the 'Advanced Subsidiary', should be graded in the same way as the full A level, and should attract half the numerical score given to the full A level in the proposed new UCAS tariff and in performance tables.

- A pilot study should be undertaken immediately to inform the design and implementation of the new AS.

SECTION 7

Unlocking potential

Recognising a wider range of achievement

7.1 This Section deals with groups of learners described as lower attainers, under-achievers, young people with learning difficulties and young people with exceptional ability. Such groupings are not intended to suggest that the solutions need to be discrete, but rather to focus on particular needs. For example, good practice for those who are underachieving or have learning difficulties could benefit all learners. Their particular needs may point up where inadequacies exist in the provision. The most important principle in addressing the special needs of these learners must be that we provide appropriate stimulation and challenges for all of them.

Lower attainers and under-achievers

7.2 Too many 16 year olds do not achieve even grade G in the GCSE, which is about the level of attainment of an average 11 or 12 year old. Some 20 per cent of our young people do not achieve this in both the core subjects of English and mathematics, and that clouds their whole future. To encourage, motivate and recognise the achievement of such young people must be a major policy objective. A range of awards has been developed, many of which are only offered locally. In Wales, the new Certificate of Educational Achievement is available for all secondary schools. In a geographically mobile society, awards that have wider currency would be a better recognition of achievement, if they can be introduced without blunting the commitment that has led to the present range of awards.

7.3 Further education has a long history of catering for learners who have been unsuccessful in school, and has developed considerable expertise in making provision which enables learners who have 'delayed' their education to re-enter the system at a later date. This is often through motivating learners in a new, more vocationally relevant activity, which may then be used as a basis from which to address the key skills of communication and the application of number. Since studies in these skills have often symbolised failure at school, they are often not addressed head on, but introduced through other studies which are motivating to the learner. Information technology can have a particular role to play in this.

Recommendations

Lower attainers

■ Criteria and procedures established by the regulatory bodies should be used for the "kitemarking" of approved awards at Entry level. The criteria would specify required standards, and amongst other things, ensure that awards are designed to offer progression to Foundation level (GCSE and GNVQ), including progression to the NCVQ units in communication, the application of number and information technology.

- All awards below the equivalent of grade G in GCSE and the Foundation level of the GNVQ, that meet these national criteria, should qualify for an Entry level National Award. (See Appendix 5.)

- In order to facilitate this accreditation, consideration should be given to implementing the powers in Section 24 of the Education Reform Act.

Under-achievers

- Students should have opportunities to take approved GNVQ units at Foundation and Intermediate levels from 14 onwards, as well as Entry level qualifications, and to take those NVQ units approved for use in schools. The increased flexibility in the revised National Curriculum after the age of 14 from September 1996 gives greater opportunities to do this.

- Further support should be given at national level to existing initiatives designed to provide motivation and opportunity among under-achievers where traditional education has not succeeded. While school will provide the centre for 14–16 year old students' continued development, education related to the adult world, with opportunities for group and project work, offers potential for those who fail to see any point or relevance to school or a traditional academic curriculum. This is especially so if a part of the student's development post-14 can be in a different environment, such as a college of further education the workplace or simulations of it. The central objective should reflect concern to serve students well in ways that are meaningful to them whilst maintaining their entitlement to the statutory curriculum.

Responding to those with learning difficulties

7.4 For those with learning difficulties, there is a need to recognise small steps of progress which for them may be a triumph. Their formal learning may be slow and hard won. In addition they need to develop accomplishments like team-working, responsiveness, and application. They should be encouraged, through recognition of achievement, to equip themselves for living independent adult lives.

Recommendations

- Courses to accredit skills for independent adult life should be developed against, or revised to meet, nationally recognised criteria for inclusion in the Section 5 list of qualifications recognised by the Government for teaching in schools pre-16, and in the possible Section 24 list for provision to full-time 16–18 students. These should be at the Entry level in the proposed National Framework, but consideration should be given to the need for further qualifications in these skills at higher levels, to provide progression routes.

- The Entry level qualifications should be available to young people with learning difficulties. The kitemarking arrangements recommended above would confirm that awards at Entry level are specified in such a way as to accredit small, worthwhile steps of progress.

Responding to the needs of those with exceptional ability

7.5 Achievement by those with exceptional ability needs recognition in all three of the academic, applied and vocational pathways. Among A level students, the traditional recognition through Special Papers (commonly known as 'S levels') has become much less used. The number of awards has halved in five years. The decline in take-up reflects resource problems in many schools in teaching small classes, and the lack of recognition given to Special Papers by universities. Many schools, colleges and universities see breadth in achievement as more valuable than further specialisation. As a result, the viability of Special Papers is at risk. The issues are, therefore, the future of Special Papers, possible alternatives to them, and what provision is appropriate for those pursuing the applied and vocational pathways.

Recommendations

- Special Papers should be regarded as one of several alternatives.

- Because Special Papers motivate some able students to excel and because some universities wish to retain them, the awarding bodies should make collaborative arrangements to ensure the continued provision of Special Papers. These should be based on existing A level subject cores, and they should be accessible to all those studying for A levels in a particular subject, not restricted to individual syllabuses as at present.

- Once reformulated, consideration should be given to recognising Special Papers through the proposed new UCAS tariff.

- As an alternative to the present approach to Special Papers, consideration should be given to externally marked extended assignments in which students research and explain a topic or issue in depth.

- Schools and universities should take advantage of opportunities available through arrangements such as Associate Student Schemes, to enable students to take units of university courses while at school or college. This will give them credit towards their undergraduate studies, as well as providing an opportunity to extend their areas of interest. With such arrangements, in a few cases it may not be unrealistic to contemplate a first degree being completed in two years.

- Schools and colleges should be encouraged to extend the range of studies available to students through additional AS or A levels, or units of GNVQs or NVQs (where appropriate opportunities can be provided) to broaden the nature of their studies. The proposal in Section 5 of this Report for a new, challenging option which combines depth with breadth of study and which would be available in all three pathways, is relevant in this context.

- Students should be encouraged to pursue opportunities outside their main curriculum to develop their personal qualities through, for example, the Duke of Edinburgh's Award Scheme, Young Enterprise or work in the community.

- For those pursuing NVQs, candidates might be encouraged to take units from NVQs in a related occupation or at a higher level; proposals for certificates underpinning the knowledge and understanding of NVQs may also be attractive to such candidates.

- Consideration should be given to developing a new AS/A level subject core for General Studies so that it will have greater standing with universities and attract a numerical score in the proposed new UCAS tariff.

- A course designed to develop critical thinking through a review of the nature of knowledge in its various forms should be developed either as a new Special Paper, or as a free-standing AS qualification, or as a new option in courses such as General Studies which lead to an A level.

7.6 This last recommendation is made in the light of interest expressed during the Review in the advantages of encouraging rigorous thinking, to widen the student's understanding of other disciplines, and to provide an opportunity to bring together gifted students pursuing different disciplines, for common study and debate.

The spiritual and moral dimension of 16–19 education

7.7 Maintained schools have a legal responsibility to provide for the spiritual, moral and cultural development of pupils, and are required to provide religious education for all, including those in the sixth form. While further education, sixth form colleges and training providers have no legal requirement to promote spiritual and moral development, these are no less relevant for their students. The spiritual and moral dimensions should be taken into account and consciously included in the curriculum and programmes of young people, and wherever possible in the design and approval of qualifications.

7.8 Spiritual and moral development has a double focus, intellectual and personal. Intellectually, young people increasingly encounter issues and experiences which raise questions of a spiritual or moral nature. These questions will frequently need resolving, often leading to action at home or in the workplace. Secondly, spiritual and moral development is integral to personal growth to adulthood. It includes care for and appreciation of the natural world, the wish to know and understand, a sense of awe and wonder, sometimes even at the simplest everyday things.

7.9 Such concerns transcend what can be achieved through qualifications alone, although these have their part to play in heightening awareness of such issues.

Recommendations

- Regulatory and awarding bodies should recognise the potential relevance of spiritual and moral issues to individual subjects, particularly when designing and approving syllabuses.

- All providers of education and training should take spiritual and moral issues into account in the design and delivery of the curriculum and programmes for young people.

Removing barriers to achievement

7.10 The national imperative is to unlock potential and to increase achievement. This will only be attained by ensuring there are no barriers of specification or assessment which unnecessarily impede access to the framework of qualifications; by ensuring that progression is available within the framework; and by minimising wastage among those who embark on a course of study leading to a qualification.

7.11 Too great a proportion of students starting on an Advanced GNVQ, and of students starting on two or three A levels, do not achieve their aim. Close analysis shows that the 'wastage' is less than the high figures often quoted. But it is still large. Measures proposed elsewhere in this Report will all be of material help. These include: a reformulated AS qualification; the reconstruction of the GNVQ through groupings of units to provide awards equivalent in size to an A level and an AS; and identifying scope for students to transfer between pathways.

7.12 Such measures will help to increase achievement, but other action is required. Particularly important is high-quality, disinterested advice on the options available to young people. Care is needed to ensure that gender and ethnic factors do not limit the opportunities available, or affect achievement.

Recommendations

■ Excellent, independent careers education and guidance should be provided to all young people on their choice of pathway, and on their potential level of achievement, recognising the central role of the local partnerships between schools, colleges and the careers service. Continued updating of knowledge should be provided to those giving advice including on issues relevant to maintaining equal opportunities.

■ The regulatory, awarding and industry lead bodies should consider the issues relating to access to qualifications as part of their work on quality assurance, including:

☐ the specification of content (audit of content for clarity, cultural and linguistic bias);

☐ assessment arrangements (special arrangements, preparation and timing of assessments);

☐ guidance to centres (for example, on equipment and learning support).

■ Awarding bodies should include criteria on accessibility and training in related issues as part of revised Codes of Practice and centre approval criteria.

■ The regulatory bodies (and other appropriate national agencies) should work together to develop a framework for monitoring and reporting nationally on candidate achievement by gender, racial origin, socio-economic group, disability or learning difficulty.

- The Government departments, regulatory and awarding bodies, Further Education Funding Councils, the Further Education Development Agency (FEDA) and other appropriate bodies should further investigate reasons for non-completion of awards (including the influence of external factors such as financial pressures, employment circumstances, personal problems, and the quality of the learning experience). They should improve the reliability of information on completion and destinations of all leavers.

- The regulatory bodies should explore (with employer bodies, Government departments and others) ways of encouraging an expansion of work experience opportunities.

SECTION 8

Action

8.1 Schools, colleges and providers of training have experienced unprecedented change in recent years. So, too, have the regulatory and awarding bodies for whom the recommendations in this Report will also involve significant additional effort if coherence is to be achieved. It is with all of these in mind that I **recommend** the following.

Recommendations

- The recommendations in this Report to strengthen qualifications are interdependent with those of the Capey Committee and of the Beaumont Review. Action on these recommendations should be co-ordinated by Government Departments to minimise the burden on institutions, the awarding bodies and providers of education and training.

- In the light of the Government's response to this Report, the DfEE, Welsh Office and Northern Ireland Office should consult with the regulatory and awarding bodies, other Government departments and the inspectorates, the Further Education Funding Councils, the Further Education Development Agency and the Teacher Training Agency on the implications of the Report and on a joint agenda for action.

- In recognition of the emphasis placed by all parties in consultation upon the need to raise national standards in the key skills of communication, the application of number and information technology, and the value attached by employers to personal and inter-personal skills, these should be included in the priorities in the joint agenda for action.

- With the continued growth of post-16 education and training, and the wider range of opportunities being offered in the applied and vocational pathways, consideration will need to be given at all levels to the curriculum that schools and colleges of different sizes can realistically provide and manage effectively within the resources available.

8.2 The recommendations in this Report have been made to raise achievement, to reduce wastage and secure good value for money. But all change involves some initial costs, particularly in terms of human effort and commitment. This is especially so in the education and training of teachers; nowhere is it more important to invest.

8.3 My final proposals therefore relate to teacher quality. The Teacher Training Agency has identified the 14–19 phase as a national priority in its recent review of continuing professional development, and is working on developing national standards to underpin the award of Qualified Teacher Status. The Government has also announced the setting up of a Further Education Staff Development Forum, supported by the Further Education Development Agency, with a remit to develop national standards and a framework for continuing professional development in the Further Education sector.

Recommendations

8.4 Further consideration should be given to:

- The case for more specific criteria for courses of initial teacher training which cover the 14–19 phase in schools.

- The implications of this Report for programmes of in-service education and training for teachers in schools.

- Whether, in the light of the outcome of the deliberations of the Further Education Staff Development Forum, there is scope for further measures for the initial and continuing training of teachers and trainers not in schools.

Appendix 1

Terms of reference and purposes of the Review

1.1 On 10 April 1995 I was invited 'to consider and advise the Secretaries of State for Education, Employment and for Wales on ways to strengthen, consolidate and improve the framework of 16–19 qualifications.'

1.2 I was asked 'to have particular regard to the need to:

- Maintain the rigour of General Certificate of Education (GCE) Advanced (A) levels.

- Continue to build on the current development of General National Vocational Qualifications (GNVQs) and National Vocational Qualifications (NVQs).

- Increase participation and achievement in education and training and minimise wastage.

- Prepare young people for work and higher education; and

- Secure maximum value for money.'

1.3 In addition to the remit, the Secretary of State for Education asked a number of questions.

- 'Is there scope for measures to achieve greater coherence and breadth of study post-16 without compromising standards; and how can we strengthen our qualifications framework further?

- Why is it that many students do not complete their courses? Can school and college resources be better used to enable young people to take full advantage of the ability to mix and match qualifications to suit their needs and abilities?

- Should we make sure that our most able pupils are stretched and suitably rewarded for excellence? And should we encourage core skills, which are already an essential part of GNVQs, as part of the programme of study for more 16–19 year olds?'

1.4 Although my remit was jointly from the Secretaries of State for Education, Employment and Wales, during my Review I have also consulted with and taken into account the interests of Northern Ireland, where the same qualifications are offered. The remit did not cover Scotland, where the education system is different, but some of the recommendations I make in this Report cover UK-wide initiatives, such as the National Record of Achievement, Modern Apprenticeships and Youth Training.

1.5 As I saw them, the purposes of the Review were to:

- Provide diversity of opportunity and informed choice for learners.

- Motivate and recognise achievement by people of all ability levels.

- Ensure standards are rigorous, challenge expectations, and encourage excellence.

■ Increase the coherence of the national qualifications framework, reduce its complexity, and make it more easily understandable by everyone.

■ Contribute to the success of young people in the world of work, and to their personal development and fulfilment.

■ Support the achievement of the new National Targets for Education and Training with their aim of providing a national workforce able to meet the international competitive challenge through high levels of skill and adaptability to change.

1.6 I presented an Interim Report in July 1995. Ministers endorsed it as the basis for work leading to this Final Report.

1.7 In both stages I have worked closely with Sir Michael Heron, the Chairman of the NCVQ, and Rudi Plaut, the Chairman of ACAC, and have benefited from the guidance of a small consultation group. We have also been supported by a team drawn from the Department for Education and Employment, the National Council for Vocational Qualifications, the School Curriculum and Assessment Authority and the Further Education Development Agency. Their names are listed below, and we record our thanks to them.

Geoff Lucas (Team Leader)	Caroline Mager
Patricia Bellas	Paul Man
Chris Boys	Tony Millns
Nancy Braithwaite	Nicola Napier
Paul Coates	Julie Sohal
Shaila Hussein	Madeleine Swords

1.8 We are grateful to our consultation group and to the many people who contributed to this Review.

National Award: Advanced Level

ABC Awarding Body*

A B Jones has received the following awards at the National Advanced Level:

GNVQ (single award)	Manufacturing	Merit
	Units Awarded†:	
	....	
	....	
AS	Business Studies	Grade B

20 August 1997   No. 1231

---

*   For the purposes of example only, showing qualifications in both the academic and applied pathways. A joint award of this sort would only be possible where awarding bodies are working in association with each other.

†   The units would be individually listed. The same practice would be adopted for A level modules on Advanced Level certificates.

Explanatory Note on Awards at the National Advanced Level

National Awards are recognised at four levels:

> Advanced

> Intermediate

> Foundation

> Entry

This certificate is an award at the Advanced level

The following are classified as being at the National Advanced Level:

i.	National Vocational Qualification (NVQ)	Level 3
ii.	General National Vocational Qualification (GNVQ)	Advanced level with grades of Distinction, Merit and Pass
	Double Award[1]	
	Single Award[2,3]	
iii.	A level	Grades A, B, C, D and E
	AS[4]	
iv.	Other qualifications recognised as Advanced include............................ (to be determined)	

---

[1]   The full GNVQ (12 units plus three key skills units) is referred to in the Report as an Applied A level (Double Award).

[2]   The proposed six unit GNVQ (including three key skills units) is called an Applied A level in the Report, and will be equal in weight to a single A level award.

[3]   At present, there is no formal GNVQ award equivalent to the AS. However, three GNVQ units are equal in weight to the AS.

[4]   An AS (Advanced Subsidiary) is equivalent to half an A level.

Appendix 3

National Award: Intermediate Level

ABC Awarding Body*

A B Jones has received the following awards at the National Intermediate Level

GNVQ **Intermediate Level**	Leisure and Tourism	Merit
	Units Awarded†:	
	....	
	....	
GCSE	Mathematics	Grade B

20 August 1997   No. 1232

---

*   For the purpose of example only.

†   The units would be individually listed.

Explanatory Notes on Awards at the National Intermediate Level

National Awards are recognised at four levels:

Advanced

Intermediate

Foundation

Entry

This certificate is an award at the Intermediate Level

The following awards are classified as being at the National Intermediate Level.

i.	National Vocational Qualification (NVQ)	Level 2 achieved by young people through Youth Training/Employment
ii.	General National Vocational Qualification (GNVQ) Part One GNVQ[1]	Intermediate level with grades of Distinction, Merit and Pass
iii.	General Certificate of Secondary Education (GCSE) GCSE short course[2]	Grades A*, A, B and C
iv.	Other qualifications recognised as Intermediate include......................(to be determined)	

---

[1]   A Part One GNVQ (Intermediate Level) is equal in weight to half a full GNVQ or two GCSEs A*–C.

[2]   A GCSE short course is equivalent to half a GCSE.

Appendix 4

National Award: Foundation Level

ABC Awarding Body*

A B Jones has received the following awards at the National Foundation Level

Part One GNVQ Foundation Level	Leisure and Tourism	Pass
	Units Awarded†:	
	....	
	....	
GCSE	Mathematics	Grade D
	Italian	Grade D

20 August 1997   No. 1233

---

*   For the purpose of example only.

†   The units would be individually listed.

Explanatory Notes on Awards at the National Foundation Level

National Awards are recognised at four levels:

Advanced

Intermediate

Foundation

Entry

This certificate is an award at the Foundation level

The following awards are classified as being at the National Foundation Level.

i.	National Vocational Qualification (NVQ)	Level I achieved by young people through Youth Training/Employment
ii.	General National Vocational Qualification (GNVQ) Part One GNVQ[1]	Foundation level with grades of Distinction, Merit and Pass
iii.	The General Certificate of Secondary Education (GCSE) GCSE short course[2]	Grades D, E, F and G
iv.	Other qualifications recognised as Foundation include..........................(to be determined)	

---

[1] A Part One GNVQ (Foundation Level) is equal in weight to half a full GNVQ or two GCSEs D–G.

[2] A GCSE short course is equivalent to half a GCSE.

Appendix 5

National Award:
Entry Level

ABC Awarding Body

A B Jones has received the following awards at the National Entry Level:

Communication	Grade A
Application of Number	Grade B
Information Technology	Grade A
Personal and Practical Skills	Grade C

20 August 1997   No. 1234

Explanatory Notes on Awards at the National Entry level

National Awards are recognised at four levels:

Advanced

Intermediate

Foundation

Entry

This certificate is an award at the Entry Level

The following awards are classified as being at the National Entry Level.

plus

either: a list of individual qualifications

or: National Entry Level Awards (Grades A, B and C) offered by .... (awarding bodies
to be determined)

These awards are part of the national framework of qualifications and lead onto GCSE, GNVQ and NVQ awards.

Appendix 6

Abbreviations used in the report

A level	Advanced level
AS	Advanced Supplementary (to be renamed 'Advanced Subsidiary')
ACAC	Awdurdod Cwricwlwm ac Asesu Cymru Curriculum and Assessment Authority for Wales
BTEC	Business and Technology Education Council
CCEA	Council for the Curriculum, Examinations and Assessment (Northern Ireland)
DfEE	Department for Education and Employment
FEDA	Further Education Development Agency
GCE	General Certificate of Education
GCSE	General Certificate of Secondary Education
GNVQ	General National Vocational Qualification
LEA	Local Education Authority
NCVQ	National Council for Vocational Qualifications
NRA	National Record of Achievement
NVQ	National Vocational Qualification
OCN	Open College Network
SCAA	School Curriculum and Assessment Authority
TEC	Training and Enterprise Council
TTA	Teacher Training Agency
UCAS	Universities and Colleges Admissions Service